BEHAVIOUR
MANAGEMENT

2nd edition

**By Peter Hook
& Andy Vass**

Cartoons:
Phil Hailstone

Published by:

Teachers' Pocketbooks
Laurel House, Station Approach,
Alresford, Hampshire SO24 9JH, UK
Tel: +44 (0)1962 735573
Fax: +44 (0)1962 733637
Email: sales@teacherspocketbooks.co.uk
Website: www.teacherspocketbooks.co.uk

*Teachers' Pocketbooks is an imprint of
Management Pocketbooks Ltd.*

Series editor – Linda Edge.

This edition published 2011.
Reprinted 2012, 2013, 2014, 2015.
ISBN 978 1 906610 43 2

E-book ISBN 978 1 908284 82 2

Previous edition 2004   ISBN 978 1 903776 59 9

© Peter Hook & Andy Vass 2004, 2011

British Library Cataloguing-in-Publication
Data – A catalogue record for this book is available
from the British Library.

Design, typesetting and graphics by Efex Ltd.
Printed in UK.

Contents

Foreword

The ideas and skills described in this book have emerged from a combined total of over 50 years' teaching experience. Most of that experience has been gained from working directly with children who exhibit challenging behaviour and from supporting colleagues in managing that behaviour.

We feel confident in stating that all the ideas and skills contained in this book will always work, with every child, every time you use them – except when they don't!

There can be no absolute guarantee when you are working with people because we are all, to some extent, unpredictable. However, having worked with over 1,000 different schools from highly challenging inner cities to leafy suburbia, LAs and other organisations across the UK, we do know that these ideas have a strong possibility of working with most children on most occasions.

Foreword

Of course, no one enjoys the luxury of getting it right every time. So what happens when things don't work?

There will always be a need for support within the processes of an effective and positive whole-school behaviour policy.

As an individual teacher, make sure you are fully aware of how the protocols in your school support you within your classroom. If you are unsure or feel they don't fit your needs then talk to colleagues and share concerns.

Remember also that talking openly about difficulties, seeking support and sharing ideas is not a sign of weakness but one of strength. Behaviour management is always more effective through collaboration.

Foreword

Developing and implementing effective whole-school policies that offer clear support on difficult issues such as the use of detentions, following up after 'exits' and how to work with children who seem 'stuck' in patterns of inappropriate behaviour despite what the school does, leads us beyond the scope of this book

We are, however, confident that the attitudes, beliefs and skills contained here will support you in becoming even better in your classroom practice. We always welcome feedback on our work and have included our email addresses on pages 126 and 127 for this purpose.

Introduction

Why manage behaviour?

Although the answer seems obvious at one level, there
are a number of goals which effective teachers seek to
achieve. These include:

1. To create a climate where learning can flourish
2. To protect basic rights of safety, learning
   and respect
3. To set the boundaries in which children can
   feel successful and achieve
4. To teach children about socially appropriate
   and acceptable choices

To achieve these goals effectively it is vital that you
also consider the *style* in which you achieve them.
Effective teachers approach their behaviour
management goals with a very positive attitude.

A positive approach

The 'positive' part of positive behaviour management means that you are working to create interactions which allow you to teach children about socially appropriate behaviour at the same time as protecting dignity and self-esteem.

Key features of a positive approach are:

- An emphasis on positive rather than negative statements
- Regular and sustained use of praise and rewards
- Teaching children the social skills they need to be successful
- Redirecting children towards success rather than highlighting their mistakes

A positive approach

POSITIVE STYLE	NEGATIVE STYLE
'Wayne, I need you to choose to face this way and listen. Thanks'	*'Wayne, stop talking and pay attention'*
'Leon, remember to walk in the corridor. Thanks'	*'Oi! Stop running'*
'Hands up to answer, Kylie. Thanks'	*'Kylie, I've told you before, stop calling out'*
'Mike, stand still and wait your turn. Thanks'	*'Mike, stop pushing or you'll go to the back'*

Relationships are the key

Building positive relationships with children is at the heart of effective behaviour management. A strong relationship connects you to your children and without that connection your ability to influence and lead them is diminished.

Relationships can be enhanced by:

- Meeting and greeting children at the door
- Showing an interest in them as individuals
- Listening to their point of view
- Giving responsibility to children
- Maintaining their dignity and self-esteem even when correcting them
- Treating them with the same level of respect that you believe you are due

Relationships are the key

If you say something often enough you end up believing it's true!

It is common practice in education to talk about 'delivering the curriculum'. Potentially this is a misleading and dangerous phrase. Learning is not something which can be 'delivered' as if it is an object like a newspaper or a pint of milk.

Learning has always occurred most naturally and therefore most effectively through the interactions between people. It happens through dialogue and relationships.

Effective teachers teach not only the formal curriculum but also social and emotional skills too.

'Your success as an educator is more dependent on positive, caring, trustworthy relationships than on any skill idea, tip or tool'
Professor Eric Jensen

About effective teachers

Teachers who manage behaviour well share the following characteristics:

Use a wide range of skills and tools

Hold realistic beliefs

Manage their emotions well

Realistic beliefs

Effective teachers come in all shapes, sizes and personalities. However, they all share certain realistic beliefs.

They understand that they cannot **control** the behaviour of children. Instead they seek to **influence** children's behaviour in these and many other ways:

- Building positive relationships
- Setting clear agendas
- Holding high expectations
- Being consistent

They also recognise that when that influence occasionally fails, they then **manage** the choices that children make. They do this by following through with the clearly defined consequences that logically follow choice.

Realistic beliefs

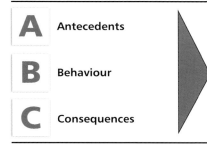

A Antecedents

B Behaviour

C Consequences

You will be most effective when you focus your attention and energy on the areas over which you have most influence – antecedents and consequences. This means building relationships and using preventative strategies followed by the consistent use of logical consequences.

Using a wide range of options

Successful teachers have a wide range of options open to them. Over their careers they collect skills and strategies and store them away for possible use.

A good metaphor for this is to imagine carrying a toolkit around with you so that ideas are always available to you. When you need something you can just dip in and find it.

Using a wide range of options

Just like real toolkits, mental ones also gather dust and fluff in the corners and split at the seams so things fall out. Take time to regularly empty out (mentally go through) your toolkit to remind yourself what's there and what hasn't proved useful.

Remember to keep observing others as they will have tools that you can pop into your toolkit too.

The person with the most options open to them in interactions will always remain calmest.

Managing your own emotions

It's important to maintain emotional balance in busy and fast-moving classrooms.

- When you are calm and rational you are most effective
- Your emotions significantly influence the classroom climate
- Positive emotions build safety and trust
- Your emotional management is a model for children

This doesn't mean you become neutral. Passion, enthusiasm and energy are essential. **NB** It's possible to overdo these too! An excess of any emotion affects the brain's ability to think rationally and sensibly.

Three Styles of Managing Behaviour

Three Styles of Managing Behaviour

It is important to establish boundaries with children of all ages. A large part of your job is to explain clearly what kinds of behaviour are acceptable and what kinds are unacceptable.

As an adult and a professional it is your right to set this agenda so that:

- A focus on learning is possible
- Children can feel safe physically and psychologically
- Everyone is treated in a dignified and respectful way

There are three broad styles of managing children's behaviour in class. Although most teachers can, at times, identify with all three styles, it is your *characteristic* style that counts.

Three Styles of Managing Behaviour

Remember:

- Your style affects the climate of relationships in class
- Your style models behaviour that children copy
- The beliefs you hold determine your style of approach

As you read about these styles, ask yourself, *'Which would I choose for my own children to experience?'*

Mrs Blitzkrieg

Believes:

- Children must be controlled
- *'Don't smile until Christmas'* is good advice
- Adults deserve respect *automatically*; children should earn it
- If one person gets away with it they'll all do it!
- Teaching is a battle that she must win all the time

Mrs Blitzkrieg

Strategies:

- Tell 'them' what to do
- Threaten them with punishments
- Send them to someone else

Outcomes:

- Poor quality relationships
- High quality stress
- Learning, risk-taking and motivation are significantly impaired

Mr Best Friend

Believes:

- Children need nurturing like buds on a flower
- Being nice and friendly makes children like you
- Planning good work and differentiating prevents misbehaviour
- Classrooms are a democracy where negotiation is key

Mr Best Friend

Strategies:

- Asking, negotiating, pleading followed by getting frustrated and cross, eg:
  'How many times do I have to tell you to be quiet?' (heavy resigned sigh)
  'Why are you still doing that?' (hurt and bewildered)
  'Wait outside. I'm fed up with you.' (emotional overload)

Outcomes:

- Uncertainty leads to insecurity
- Leadership of the classroom is 'up for grabs'
- Learning, risk-taking and motivation are significantly impaired

Tough Care

Believes:

- A teacher's job is to set boundaries
- A child's job is to test them
- Children making mistakes about their behaviour is normal and healthy
- Children should be helped to experience achievement
- Caring means saying *'No'* and meaning *'No'* at the right time
- There is always more to a child than the problems they present

Tough Care

Strategies:

- Treats behaviour as a choice made
- Holds children accountable for their choices
- Creates a culture of praise that focuses on what children do well
- Redirects children towards success
- Applies sanctions if needed but not grudges
- Looks to teach social skills to lead to better choices

Outcomes:

- Children learn boundaries whilst retaining dignity
- The teacher is both leader and coach in the classroom
- Learning, risk-taking and motivation are significantly enhanced

Reflective activity

- On a scale of 0 – 10 (where 10 is the best it can be and 0 is Mrs Blitzkrieg), to what extent does your practice reflect the 'tough care' approach?
- How come that number and not 0?
- What do you already do that is successful?
- What are the smallest things that you could and would do to increase your score by one point?

Introduction

 Three Styles of Management

 Getting the Basics Right ◀

 Eight Core Principles

 Ten Step Discipline Plan

 Developing the Toolkit

 A Framework to Underpin Practice (4Rs)

 Reflective Summary

Getting the Basics Right

Influence rather than control

Remember - you *CANNOT* directly control the behaviour of your children.

You *CAN* control some, but not all, of the antecedents (see page 15) such as:

- Where and how you display children's work
- How you greet children
- How you initiate conversations
- How you use seating plans and establish entry routines, etc

You have little control over other antecedents such as poor housing, lack of appropriate parenting skills, etc.

You do, however, have 100% control over how you choose to respond emotionally to child behaviour. By controlling your response, you can *influence* children's behaviour but you cannot control it.

Sanctions

The most important message here is **sanctions do not change behaviour**.

- Effective sanctions simply **limit** behaviour long enough to allow you to reward the new, desired behaviour

- It is not the severity of sanctions that makes them effective limiters; it is their inevitability – the certainty that you *will* do something

- Classroom sanctions are best arranged as a hierarchy, eg:
  - Warning
  - Move seat
  - Five minutes behind at the end of lesson
  - Parents/carers informed
  - Exit classroom

- Sanctions should always be applied as a choice – *'Sean, if you continue to stop Marcus working you will be choosing a warning.'* – and therefore as a logical consequence of the child's action

Rewards

The most important message here is **rewards change behaviour**.

- Emotional feedback is the most effective form of reward – smiles, thank yous, and gestures such as 'thumbs up'
- Tangible rewards (stars, stickers and stamps) are not effective in the long term unless they are linked to emotional feedback
- Once given, rewards should never be taken away from the child – if they make a poor choice after receiving a reward then apply the appropriate sanction
- Rewards must be given out fairly and not used as 'bribes' with the most troublesome children
- 16-year-old children respond to stars and stickers as well as six-year-old children provided they are given out in an age-appropriate way

Seating

Always have a clearly established seating plan for all of your children.

- As soon as your children agree to sit in your seating plan, they have agreed that you can set the key agendas in the room
- Don't spread all the most difficult children around the room – they will simply start shouting to each other across the room
- If you choose to sit children in groups, you must accept a certain level of social behaviour
- Change your seating plan every so often to vary working pairs and maximise learning
- Make sure that children with poor concentration sit near you and away from obvious distractions such as windows

Positioning

Where you position yourself in the classroom can have a significant impact on your effectiveness.

Consider these ideas:

- Don't always teach from the front – if you spend all your time at the front of the classroom then the rest of the room will become the children's territory
- Move around the room – establish the whole room as your territory
- When you are 'up front', position yourself towards one of the front corners – you can scan the whole room more easily from here than in the centre
- When you are working with an individual or group, position yourself so that you can look up and scan the rest of the room easily
- Move over to a child when you want to correct their behaviour rather than trying to intervene from the other side of the room
- Don't invade a child's 'personal space'. If you get too close, you will dramatically increase the chances of turning a discipline transaction into a confrontation

Begin and end positively

Lesson beginning and ending routines are an essential part of effective behaviour management. They are the points at which you either set the social tone for this lesson or pre-frame the agenda for next lesson.

- Greet children at the start of a lesson with a smile and have an activity ready for them to engage in, thus setting a positive social and work agenda. This is particularly important for children who find it hard to settle or who like to challenge teachers

- At the end of the lesson, if all has gone reasonably well, tell the class what you particularly liked about the lesson. Don't dwell on what didn't work; focus on what went well

- Ideally, dismiss children by standing at the classroom door and sending them out two or three at a time. This helps to 'filter' them into busy corridors

- Say something positive to every child as they go past you – even just a smile and a *'goodbye'* helps

Establish a climate of 'good manners'

Good manners cost nothing and are the social 'glue' that, day-to-day, forms cohesive groups.

- Demonstrate through your own behaviour what appropriate social behaviours you expect from your children. Simple examples are:
  - Always saying *'Please'* and *'Thank you'*
  - Holding doors open for children
  - Greeting children with a smile and *'Good morning'*
  - Saying *'Thank you'* when a child holds a door open for you
  - Saying *'Excuse me'* when you want to pass between two children
- *Gently* correct children who forget good manners: *'John, remember to choose to say 'Please' when you ask for something.'*
- If you have to break off a conversation with a child to deal with another child's inappropriate behaviour, apologise first: *'I'm sorry, I just need to have a word with Kieran. I'll be back in a moment.'*

Invest to receive

Invest to receive

There is a basic law of human relationships that says, *'If you want to receive something it is better to give it first.'* This principle applies at all levels in your interactions with children.

- If you show respect towards your children you are much more likely to be treated with respect yourself

- If you choose to respond to children in a calm, rational manner you are less likely to be met with confrontation

- If you take time to understand your children as people rather than little 'learning machines' you are much more likely to be able to establish good working relationships

- If you demonstrate a firm but fair approach to discipline you are much more likely to have children who comply with your behavioural expectations

- If you greet them with a smile and a friendly *'Good morning'* when you call the register you are much more likely to get a friendly reply than the usual grunt

Introduction

 Three Styles of Management

 Getting the Basics Right

 Eight Core Principles

 Ten Step Discipline Plan

 Developing the Toolkit

 A Framework to Underpin Practice (4Rs)

 Reflective Summary

Eight Core Principles

Why principles?

Effective leadership is principle-centred. Making day-to-day decisions about managing behaviour within a framework of principles helps you to remain more positive in your practice.

In a busy classroom or playground you have to respond to events quickly. Matching your response to clear principles increases your consistency and fairness.

Principles bring personal responsibility. All of us act hastily against our principles from time to time, eg being 'snappy' with a child. When we do, it is the principles that lead us to reconnect and repair the relationship.

The following eight principles reflect good practice in all phases of teaching.

1. Plan for good behaviour

Planning for good behaviour balances two crucial elements, **prevention** and **reduction**.

The most effective behaviour management actively limits the opportunities for, or likelihood of, inappropriate behaviour occurring.

However, when it does (as it will!) occur, reducing friction or potential conflict is crucial. To do this effectively you need to deliberately choose a strategy from your toolkit rather than react in an unplanned or emotionally-driven way.

1. Plan for good behaviour

Prevention

Because preventative strategies will support you in your effectiveness, it is valuable to develop your own 'resource bank' of ideas.

Make three headings on a piece of paper. Add as many strategies as you can in each column and join with colleagues to extend the lists.

Keep the lists to hand – perhaps in your planner – and refer to them to help build a preventative climate in your class.

CURRICULUM	ORGANISATION	INTER-PERSONAL
learning styles	seating plans	meeting & greeting

1. Plan for good behaviour

Reduction

Positive behaviour management requires that emotional 'heat' is reduced quickly and effectively. This obviously applies to you too!

Recognise the choices you have available, remain rational in your thinking and respond in a planned way by drawing on skills from your toolkit. Give only the bare minimum of attention possible to the child who misbehaves. Do this by directing them to the behaviour you want rather than what you wish them to stop doing.

'Michael, I need you to face the front and listen now. Thank you,' is briefer and more effective than: *'Michael, why are you turning round? You shouldn't be talking when I am – you should be listening.'*

Notice how the child is redirected towards success rather than focusing on the mistake.

2. Separate the (inappropriate) behaviour from the child

In addressing **inappropriate behaviour** you should always make it clear that it is the behaviour and not the person that you are critical of.

Remember:

- What they do is not the same as who they are
- Labelling the person as 'bad' often confirms a poor self-image
- Children live up (or down) to the image you hold of them
- Children need hope to change their behaviour

The language of choice (page 46) makes it easier to uphold this principle. Treating errors as a poor choice:

- Limits the mistake to one context only
- Implies that success is possible (better choice) next time

2. Separate the (inappropriate) behaviour from the child

Appropriate behaviour, however, should always be associated with the person. When children make good choices about their behaviour, your feedback should carry the message, *'You're the kind of person who.......'*

Examples:

'Including Danielle in your game at playtime shows how kind you are, Michelle. Thank you.'

'The way you've tackled this course work has really demonstrated your commitment, Steve. That's impressive.'

3. Use the language of choice

Exercising choice is one of the most powerful motivational forces human beings experience. When you act as if your children choose their own behaviour you become strongly empowered and so do they.

Much of the tension and conflict occurring in schools results from power struggles between the child and the adult. This is not simply an adolescent phenomenon, although it appears more widely at that time.

Managing behaviour has three phases:

1. Giving children choices about their behaviour within fair rules
2. Influencing them to make appropriate choices
3. Applying the consequences of their choices (rewards and sanctions)

3. Use the language of choice

At first the language of choice may seem awkward. Practise it and personalise it until it flows naturally.

Consider the profound difference between these two instructions:

'Wayne, if you don't stop talking I'll move you over here on your own.'

'Wayne, if you choose to keep talking while I'm teaching, you'll be choosing to sit here on your own. Make a better choice now. Thanks.'

The first says, 'If you don't do what I want now, I'll make you do this'. It is a direct threat and a challenge many children cannot resist meeting.

The second says, 'You are responsible for your behaviour. I want you to make this choice because it protects the basic right to teach (see page 108) but if you don't, then you will have chosen this sanction'. It offers a limited range of choices but crucially gives the child the chance to move to more successful behaviour.

4. Focus on primary behaviours

Primary behaviours are those which require intervention by you because they impede the classroom agenda.

Many children when corrected will engage in **secondary behaviours**. These are ways of diverting attention from the mistake they've made and allow them to 'de-stress' and feel better.

When you react to secondary behaviours you are 'buying-in' to the diversion and losing sight of why you spoke to the child in the first place. You also run the risk of being 'wound up'!

There are two types of secondary behaviour, non-verbal and verbal.

4. Focus on primary behaviours

Non-verbal

These are the sighs, pouts, hair-tossing, moans, eyebrow raises etc that children do when being corrected.

Effective skills:

1. Completely ignore the body language. After a while it just stops!
2. Move the child away from an audience if needed
3. Take up a relaxed posture (it will help you stay calm)
4. Reaffirm your message calmly, clearly and assertively
5. Ask them to choose better behaviour
6. Set them back on task

4. Focus on primary behaviours

Verbal

These are the 'justifications' given for the behaviour or alternative diversionary tactics:
'I was only talking about the work (heavy sigh)'
'They're doing it too (why pick on me?)'
'Other teachers let us sit with our friends (we like them!)'

Effective skill: *'maybe... and...'*

- Validate their perception of events: *'Maybe...'*
- Redirect them to what you want them to be doing: *'and I still need you to...'*

'Maybe you were and I still need you to face this way and listen. Thanks.'
'Maybe they are and I still need you to put your pen down. Thanks.'
'Maybe they do and in this class we have a seating plan. Choose to sit over there. Thanks.'

4. Focus on primary behaviours

You will need to practise hard to be able to say *'maybe...and'* rather than *'maybe... but'*. However, this is a **very** powerful strategy.

- It defuses conflict by seeming to agree with the child
- The use of *'and'* makes the redirection feel OK to comply with
- It minimises the potential for you getting into arguments
- It allows you to move on and regain the momentum of the lesson

Remember:

- Use a matter-of-fact tone of voice
- Make the statement flow seamlessly
- Use 'compliance time' immediately afterwards (see page 92)
- Whatever follows the *'and'* is what you want them to do

5. Actively build trust and support

All mutually supportive relationships are built on trust.

It would be a mistake to assume that simply being pleasant and friendly with children wins their trust. You have to demonstrate over time your trustworthiness to earn the trust of your class(es).

There are many ways you can do this:

- Setting and reinforcing clear boundaries
- Being consistent in your approach and expectations
- Keeping your promises (to keep them safe, help them learn, maintain respect, etc)
- Being sensitive to individuals
- Paying attention to detail (remembering names, greeting them in and beyond the classroom, lending pens, etc)

5. Actively build trust and support

Rapport is the way in which you connect to another person. Being connected to a child is the only way in which you can influence them effectively.

You can build rapport by:

- Positive non-verbal signals such as smiles, nods and thumbs up
- Using a high ratio of praise and positive comments
- Showing that you listen to concerns and viewpoints
- Giving lots of evidence-based praise

5. Actively build trust and support

Example:

'You've used paragraphs correctly, proofread well and presented your work neatly. Excellent! Well done!'

You can develop connections and agreement with children quickly by simply stating what is happening at the time:

Example:

'Kyle, you're out of your seat.'
'Michelle, you haven't started yet.'

6. Model the behaviour you wish to see

Although this may seem obvious, it is worth reinforcing that *your* behaviour is the most significant influence in the classroom.

Children are in the process of acquiring the social skills to make successful choices about their behaviour. They need you as a role model.

You do not have to be perfect in your behaviour. Being a normal human being who makes mistakes (and apologises for them) is in itself a powerful model.

What is important is how well you model the correct behaviours the *majority* of the time.

The worst accusation a child can make when being corrected is, *'Well you do it!'*

6. Model the behaviour you wish to see

Key behaviour	Example
Maintaining dignity and respect	Even when the child has misbehaved
Resolving conflict	Apply sanctions without grudges
Protecting safety (psychological and/or physical)	Avoid sarcasm or put downs and challenge children who use them
Making mistakes is part of learning	Deal with them as choices that didn't work
Managing emotions	Use compliance time (page 92) and time out to help reduce arousal

7. Follow up on issues that count

You have to make decisions as to what counts. Primarily the three basic rights described in the 4Rs chapter (page 106) always count. On a day-by-day basis other things will count too.

The intention of this principle is to guide you away from the notion of 'manic vigilance' whereby you try to spot every infringement and deal with it. You will quickly become exhausted and also create a very stressful climate in your class.

The crucial thing is that you make deliberate choices in your leadership of the class.

- What can you ignore and for how long?

- When is the best moment to deal with this?

- What is the least intrusive skill that gets things back on track?

8. Reconnect and repair relationships

You can only influence children's behaviour when you have some connection to them. Applying a necessary sanction as a result of their behaviour choice may create some tension or resentment.

You should seek to reconnect positively to a child as soon as possible after correcting them. Certainly, you should always have a positive chat *before* they leave the class even if it's just to smile and say *'goodbye'*.

8. Reconnect and repair relationships

Reconnecting to a child usually doesn't require anything more than a simple skill.

You can achieve this non-verbally or verbally, eg:

• Smiling as you look over at them or, *'How are you getting on? Do you need a hand?'*

Remember this skill connects directly into modelling good behaviour. You are the adult in this relationship and are paid to teach children appropriate skills and behaviours.

Reflective activity

Take each principle in turn and explore it with the following questions:

- WHAT?
- HOW?
- WHY?

Example: Separate (inappropriate) behaviour from the child.

WHAT does this mean to you? WHAT do you understand about this principle?

HOW do you or HOW will you show its use consistently in your work?

WHY would you bother to develop this principle? WHY would it allow you to be even more effective?

Introduction

 Three Styles of
Management

 Getting the
Basics Right

 Eight Core
Principles

 Ten Step
Discipline Plan ◀

 Developing
the Toolkit

 A Framework
to Underpin
Practice (4Rs)

 Reflective
Summary

Ten Step
Discipline Plan

The ten step plan

Each time you deal calmly but assertively with inappropriate behaviour in your classroom, you add value to your leadership. At times this is easier said than done!

What really helps is feeling confident in your ability to respond positively and appropriately to a range of challenging behaviours that may:

a. Not initially respond to your interventions
b. Increase in severity

It is also important that you are as consistent in your practice as possible to avoid accusations of being 'unfair'.

Effective teachers appear very confident in their practice. Their confidence comes from having a clear plan that allows them to respond calmly to the least and most serious incidents.

This chapter offers you a ten step plan to support your discipline process. It is not definitive nor the answer to all problems. Explore, refine and above all personalise it to provide structure and support for your classroom.

Step 1 – catch them being good

An encouraging and supportive climate needs an emphasis on positive comments.

- Whenever possible, focus first on those children who are choosing to be compliant rather than those who are choosing not to behave

- Publicly praise children who are on task whilst ignoring those children who are off task. Be specific in what you are praising: *'Well done, I like the way you are all sitting quietly and looking at me. Thank you'*

- If the off-task children focus back on task, praise them

- If some children do not return to task, redirect by gently repeating your directions

Step 2 – use positive cueing

Positive cueing seeks to use children behaving well as models or reminders to those children who are not. It links well with step 1 as:

- You are catching children being good, and giving recognition
- You are redirecting children back to successful and appropriate behaviour

Example:
Praise children who are making good choices near your off-task target child. Say Nicola is not following the directions to put her pen down and look at you but Jarrell, sitting next to her, is:

- You say: *'Jarrell, thanks for putting down your pen and looking at me. Well done'*
- Nicola, on this prompt, puts down her pen and looks at you
- You acknowledge this by smiling and saying: *'Thanks Nicola'*

Step 3 – use physical proximity

Your ability to regulate your physical proximity to groups and individuals is a key part of your 'toolkit'.

Example:
You notice that Mark is off task so you start to move among children, getting gradually closer to Mark but praising on-task behaviour of other children as you go.

- *'Wayne,* (three desks away from Mark) *thanks for working quietly'*
- You continue to move towards Mark and continue praising
- *'Martine,* (a desk away) *I like the way you're working so well on your own'*
- As soon as Mark is on task, you switch your attention and praise on to him

Step 4 – use questions to refocus

Seemingly casual questions can be a very powerful way of unobtrusively refocusing an off-task child.

Example:
You gently approach one or more children but pay no attention to their off-task behaviour.

- You simply ask a gently redirective question: *'How's it going? Do you need any help?'; 'Sylvia, do you need me to check how you're doing so far?'* etc

- You then leave the refocused child with an expectation of continued compliance: *'I'll pop back in a minute and see how far you've got'*

Step 5 – privately repeat directions

Giving the child a *brief*, private direction followed by a few seconds to enable the child to refocus their behaviour is particularly effective with children who respond badly to public reprimands.

Example:
You notice Kyle has stopped focusing on his work.

- You quietly move to his side and say: *'Kyle, I need you to go back to answering these questions, thanks'*

- You don't expect instant compliance, but move away to give him a few seconds to modify his behaviour

- When Kyle is back on task you move over and positively reinforce the improved behaviour

Step 6 – acknowledge and redirect

Rather than getting involved in argumentative or secondary behaviours, smart teachers use acknowledgement followed by redirection.

Example:
You notice Tiffany talking with Jade rather than being on task.

- You move over to them: *'Jade, Tiffany. I need you back on task now, thanks'*

- Tiffany replies: *'I was only asking Jade what we've got next'*

- You respond with: *'I realise you need to know what lesson you've got next and you can ask her at the end of the lesson* (acknowledgement) *and right now I need you back on task* (redirection), *thanks'* (expect compliance)

Step 7 – give a clear rule reminder

Private, assertive reminders of your classroom rules can be
a very effective, non-confrontational strategy. By
referring to the rules as 'our rules' you are, to a
certain extent, de-personalising your discipline
transaction. It takes away the *'Because I say so'*
element that gives some children the chance to
escalate off-task behaviour into open challenge.

Example:
* *'Charlene, remember that our rule for
  answering questions is hands up. I'd like
  you to follow that now, thanks'*

Step 8 – give a clear choice

Articulating the consequences of continued, inappropriate choices puts the locus of control and responsibility firmly within the child. Equally, as with Step 7, it considerably reduces the *'Because I say so'* element.

Example:
You notice Maria out of her seat again talking to Carl.

- You move over to her and calmly and assertively state the consequences of continued inappropriate behaviour
- *'Maria, I need you to choose to stay in your seat* (restate directions). *If you choose not to you will be choosing to see me at the end of the lesson* (state consequences). *Back to your seat now, thanks'* (expect compliance)

Step 9 – use agreed consequences

If the child continues to make poor choices, you can apply your agreed consequences, each time expecting compliance.

Example:

- *'Maria, you've chosen to see me at the end of the lesson* (apply consequences). *Back to your seat now, thanks'* (expect compliance)

- If the child continues to make poor choices or openly refuses to cooperate, you may calmly repeat Steps 8 and 9 working through your hierarchy of consequences

- When the child complies, repair the relationship by praising

Step 10 – use exit strategies

If children continue to significantly prevent you from teaching and/or other children from learning, it is appropriate that they are exited from the classroom using your school's agreed procedures.

- Usually, an exit should be given as a choice (*'Mark, you've chosen to be exited.'*) and always preceded by other strategies

- Use exit strategies calmly and assertively with the clear message that the exit is being used because of the child's poor choices. (*'Sean, you are continually choosing to…'*)

- Always follow up an exit by talking with the child and planning for better choices next time

Exit considerations

An exit is clearly the most serious of your classroom-based interventions. It should be used with discretion to retain impact. The only occasion that an exit is not preceded by a series of strategies would be if the child's behaviour endangers safety.

Remember, using an exit in this way is not a sign of failure. It is a legitimate strategy and should be part of your discipline plan.

Because an exit is serious there are a number of considerations that should be given to the process.

Exit considerations

It is best if agreement is reached over these ideas through whole staff discussion:

- What sorts of behaviours necessitate exit?
- What sorts of language patterns are appropriate during exit?
- How do you get the child out? (there are age and safety aspects here)
- What if they refuse to go?
- How and where can you seek help?

Exit considerations

- Where does the child go?
- What happens to them there?
- What is the role of the 'receiving' adult?
- What records are to be kept?
- Who should be informed?
- What actions are triggered if exit occurs regularly?

Exit considerations

An exit is only the initial consequence; therefore your role as initiating teacher is also crucial.

Following an exit you should meet with the child as soon as possible to:

- Discuss making better choices next time
- Demonstrate that you hold no grudges and next time is a fresh start
- Arrange for the work missed to be done
- Teach the child any new skills needed to be able to make better choices next time
- Reconnect and repair the relationship

It is also important to inform parents and your key stage co-ordinator, head of department or head of year as appropriate.

Introduction

 Three Styles of Management

 Getting the Basics Right

 Eight Core Principles

 Ten Step Discipline Plan

 Developing the Toolkit ◀

 A Framework to Underpin Practice (4Rs)

 Reflective Summary

Developing the Toolkit

The metaphor of the toolkit

The metaphor of a toolkit is very appropriate for classroom management. It is a way of recognising that there isn't one solution or fixed approach.

A simple maxim is: *When what you do isn't working, stop doing it and do something different.*

Effective teachers assess the nature and context of the situation before dipping into their toolkit and selecting the most appropriate skill or strategy to use.

Honing your tools

To develop as an effective teacher, it is not enough to read through a list of strategies and remember them.

Just like real tools they require regular use. You have to practise with them to acquire the skills, the dexterity and the decision-making processes that distinguish the craftsperson from the DIY enthusiast.

Take time to:

- Reflect on your skills
- Take feedback and keep learning
- Rehearse the verbal and non-verbal language skills until they become genuinely your own
- Give yourself credit for your success and achievements

Expectation of compliance

All your strategies are far more likely to be successful if you **believe** they will work and act accordingly.

It is a way of demonstrating confidence and assertiveness throughout your interactions with children. In this way children recognise that you are the leader in the classroom.

You can convey expectation through:

1. Verbal language
2. Body language

Verbal expectation

Use *'thank you'* rather than *'please'* at the end of a direction.

eg *'Shaquib,* (pause) *pen down and facing this way. Thanks.'*

Finishing a discipline transaction with *'Thanks'* is effectively saying to the child:
'I'm so sure that you will comply with my request that I'm thanking you for it already.'

'Thanks' also triggers a greater sense of obligation to comply and gives a clear element of closure to the interaction.

Body language expectation (compliance time)

Having given a positive verbal instruction ending with *'Thanks'* it is important not to 'over-dwell' on the discipline transaction. The following actions help:

1. Drop eye contact with the child
2. Turn away and engage with other children
3. Move to a child who is working well and spend more time with them giving praise

By doing this you are effectively giving subtle and very powerful messages:

- I'm confident you will do the correct thing
- I also trust you to make the correct choice
- I'm so sure that you will comply that I don't have to stay to make sure
- See how children get praise and positive attention? Remember this for next time

Deliberate ignoring

This is NOT the same as simply ignoring difficult behaviour. It's about your management decisions. As part of your toolkit you need to decide:

- What things can be ignored and for how long
- When they can be ignored. (Often 'up front' with whole class attention is a good time)
- What you will do next if ignoring doesn't work

Deliberate ignoring

There are two types of ignoring:

1. **Brutal:** When you simply ignore what's going on and, ideally simultaneously, acknowledge children doing the right thing, eg putting their hands up.

2. **Prefaced:** When you give a brief instruction before ignoring, eg *'When you're in your seat with your hand up then I'll help'* followed by turning away and ignoring.

Give advice before warnings

A simple, non-confrontational technique is to help children correct their actions
by giving them information about how the world works. Giving 'advice' in this way,
especially with younger children, acts as a friendly warning, as well as an opportunity
to take responsibility before you try resorting to more direct methods.

Example:

- *'Carl, if you hit other children, they won't want to play with you'*

- *'Cindy, paint dries out if you don't put the lid back on'*

- *'Kylie, if we don't put the books away neatly then we won't be able to find them easily next time'*

K.I.S.S. (Keep it Short and Simple)

It is sometimes tempting when we are faced with repeated, low-level misbehaviour to vent our frustration by going into 'monologue mode'.

Short, simple directions enable children to:

- Focus on the key issue
- Identify the problem
- Resolve the problem

K.I.S.S. (Keep it Short and Simple)

Example:

Compare...
'John, you've forgotten to put your homework on my desk again. If you spent less time chatting with your friends and more time paying attention to the important things in life you might get on better in class. Just come back here and put your book where it is supposed to be.'

...with
'John. Homework on my desk. Thanks.'

Simply describe the problem

Giving a short description without apportioning any blame is a powerful, non-confrontational way of treating misbehaviour as simply a mistake that can be easily corrected.

It is very similar to K.I.S.S. but goes further by directly inviting the child to solve the problem.

Examples:
- *'I can hear lots of answers being called out but I can't see who's saying them. What would help?'*
- *'There seems to have been a lot of paper dropped on the floor and we need the room tidy for the next class. I'd like your help in sorting it out, thanks'*
- *'Sean, you seem to have spilled some paint on the floor. What do you need to do now?'*

Use positive language

Use *'Do'* rather than *'Don't'* in your interactions with children.
Telling children what you want them to do will always be more effective than telling them what you want them to stop doing because the human brain finds it easier to process positives than negatives.

Examples:

- *'Carla, I'd like you to choose to sit down now. Thank you'* is much more likely to be successful than, *'Carla, don't walk about the room please'*

- *'Hands up if you want to say something,'* will be more successful than, *'Don't shout out,'* especially if you model it by simultaneously holding up your own hand

Use 'Either... or...' choices

Be clear about the choices that children have in your classroom. Give a clear choice of either complying or receiving the agreed consequence (see 'sanctions' page 31).

Either...or... choices reduce the chances of the discipline transaction becoming confrontational.

Example:
- *'Javed, you can either choose to sit down or you will be choosing to stay behind for five minutes.'*

Use only one formal warning

Do not use repeated formal warnings as it encourages children to continue to 'push the boundaries' – *'Luke, this is your third final warning,'* is not effective!

Example:
Kyle is constantly shouting across the room during an on-task phase of the lesson.

- You go over to Kyle and preface your formal warning with a clear choice: *'Kyle, if you continue to shout out you'll be choosing a warning'*

- If Kyle persists in his poor choice of behaviour, clarify his choice and expect compliance: *'Kyle, you've chosen a warning. Back on task now. Thank you'*

- If he chooses to ignore this warning, move on to the next sanction in your hierarchy: *'Kyle, if you shout out again you will be choosing to move your seat. Back on task now. Thank you'*

Allow for 'compliance time'

Unless there is a risk of children harming themselves or others, do not insist on instant compliance. Allowing a little 'compliance time' reduces confrontation and allows older children to 'save face' in front of their peers.

Example:
Wayne is out of his seat and is preventing other children from working.

- You intervene by saying: *'Wayne, I'd like you to choose to sit down. Thank you.'* Wayne 'tuts' and rolls his eyes

- You choose not to react to his posturing but immediately turn your attention back to on-task children

- A few seconds later, Wayne strolls back to his seat and you reinforce his better choice by going over to him and saying: *'Thanks for choosing that, Wayne. Do you need a hand?'*

Deal with 'You can't make me!' with agreement

When children say, *'You can't make me!'* many teachers feel instantly disabled and frequently give way to their own inner voice that says, *'Oh, can't I! We'll see about that!'* with the inevitable result of a confrontation.

The reality is that you can't *make* children do anything. We can use this fact to our advantage by agreeing with the child and expecting them to do it anyway.

Deal with 'You can't make me!' with agreement

Example:
Mandy and her friends have not responded to your formal warning and are still chatting instead of finishing their work.

- You go over to them and say: *'If you choose not to get on with your work then you will be choosing to move seats'*

- Mandy responds with: *'You can't make us do the work!'*

- You calmly respond with: *'You're right Mandy, I can't make you and I'd like you to choose to have it finished in 5 minutes, thanks.'* You then turn away and leave them a few seconds' 'compliance time'

'When... then...' ('Grandma's Rule')

Simply stated, 'Grandma's Rule' goes like this: **'When** *you've eaten your peas* **then** *you can have your pudding.'* This conditional statement can be used in a wide variety of classroom situations.

Examples:

- *'Martine, when you've got your hand up then I'll answer your question'*

- *'Daryl, when you're in your seat then I'll check your work with you'*

- *'Petrea, when I've listened to what Keith has to say then I'll listen to your side of the story'*

- *'Sinead, when you've finished these questions then you can go back and sit with Winston'*

Use explanatory 'I' messages

The use of the personal pronoun 'I' adds significantly to the effectiveness of a discipline transaction. An 'I' message acknowledges that there is a problem and opens the way towards a solution without blame or conflict.

An effective 'I' statement has four parts:

1. A brief description of the behaviour.
2. The effect of this behaviour.
3. Your feelings.
4. The new desired behaviour.

Explanatory 'I' messages

Example:
Carla is shouting out to get your attention whilst you are offering support to Billy.

- You temporarily break off from Billy: *'I'm sorry Billy, and I just need a quick word with Carla'*

- You turn to Carla and calmly say to her: *'Carla, when you shout at me* (behaviour) *it stops me helping Billy* (effect) *and I feel frustrated* (your feelings). *I'd like you to choose to wait until I've helped Billy and then I'll come and help you.'* (new, desired behaviour)

Use a 5-W follow-up routine

This is a powerful conversation framework that can be used when following up with children at the end of a lesson.

- *What did you do?* Ask the child to describe their behaviour. If they say, *'I don't know,'* then calmly and factually describe their behaviour to them
- *Why did you do it?* This gives the child the chance to explain their actions. If they simply say, *'I don't know,'* then accept this and move on
- *What rule did it break?* Make sure that they know why you decided the behaviour was unacceptable
- *What would be a better choice next time?* In effect, you are teaching the child more appropriate social behaviour for next time
- *What can I do to help you?* There are lots of alternative ways you can support children in making better choices next time

Avoid over-dwelling on discipline transactions

Some children learn that they can get as much undivided teacher attention as they want simply by displaying low-level disruptive behaviour. Other children feel threatened if you keep your emotional 'spotlight' focused on them following an intervention. Either way, the most effective strategy is to move your attention away from the poor, undesirable behaviour as soon as possible.

Once you have intervened with a child, move away or change your focus as quickly as possible. Turning away and breaking eye contact when you are up front in class, or moving away as you are working the room is a subtle yet very powerful way of conveying:

- The transaction is over and there's no more to be said
- You are confident that the pupil will follow the direction
- You expect them to comply
- You care about their self-esteem and will turn the spotlight off quickly
- You do not dwell or add 'heat' to your directions

Tactical use of 'the pause'

It takes time to stop doing something and think about, understand and then do something else. You are more likely to achieve compliance from children if you deliberately allow time for this process.

Putting in a pause after you call the pupil's name and before you give the direction helps to gain and then sustain the attention. It's also OK to have to repeat a pupil's name a couple of times.

Example:
Waquib has drifted off and is gazing out of the window at a crucial point in your up-front session.

- Hardly interrupting your flow at all you simply say, *'Waquib'* (one second pause) *'This way, thanks,'* and immediately return your attention to class. As soon as you notice him looking at you, you reinforce his new, desired behaviour with a quick *'thumbs up'* gesture and a smile

Double 'what' questions

A very effective element of behaviour management is to use refocusing questions. These challenge the child to actively accept responsibility without blaming.

In class, questions asking, 'Why?' rarely lead to useful information. It is better to refocus by casually asking, 'What?'

Example:

T: *'Michael, I notice you're out of your seat. What are you doing?'*

M: *'Nothing'*

T: *'What should you be doing'?*

M: *'I dunno!'*

T: *'You should be finishing the questions. Choose to get back to work now. Thanks'*

The broken record effect

For those children who begin to question or challenge it can be very effective simply to repeat your directions two or three times accompanied by a blocking action with your open hand.

T: *'Chris, pen down and looking this way. Thanks'*

C: *'But, I...'*

T: *'Choose to put your pen down, Chris. Thanks'*

C: *'I was only...'*

T: *'Pen down... pen down... Thanks'*

Rule of three

Many teachers get frustrated by having to repeat their instructions several times to the same children without any noticeable effect. If you continue to repeat the same things over and over again, you are teaching the child that they don't have to take any notice of you!

A useful rule of thumb is three repetitions of the direction. You should then follow this up with a consequential choice.

Example:
'Tunde, I've asked you twice to stay in your seat. If you choose to leave your seat without permission, you'll be choosing a warning. Make a better choice. Thanks'

Use 'time out' or 'cool-off time'

On those occasions where children seem to be having an off-day or simply do not respond to a variety of low-level interventions, using formal 'time out' is valuable. Time out provides a *brief* time away from others to settle and calm. It is a chance to reflect and make better choices on rejoining the class.

In KS 1 & 2, this would generally be within the classroom and last about three minutes. Having a display of photographs of the class making appropriate choices adds value to the time out. In KS 3 & 4, it is usually outside the room in the corridor and should be no more than five minutes.

Always precede re-entry into the class by checking that the child is aware of, and is prepared to make, more appropriate choices. Look to catch them making those choices as quickly as possible and praise them.

Introduction

 Three Styles of
Management

 Getting the
Basics Right

 Eight Core
Principles

 Ten Step
Discipline Plan

 Developing
the Toolkit

 A Framework
to Underpin
Practice (4Rs)

 Reflective
Summary

The 4Rs –
A Framework to
Underpin Practice

The 4Rs framework

In managing your classroom effectively, you will need to set a clear agenda for the children that guides and supports them in making appropriate choices about their behaviour.

One of the most effective frameworks within which to do this is called the 4Rs (Hook & Vass 2000, 2002). The 4Rs are:

1. **Rights** – basic rights are safety, learning and fair treatment
2. **Responsibilities** – emotional and social growth are enhanced through accountability
3. **Rules** – describe behaviours which protect rights
4. **Routines** – agreed actions that support smooth organisation

The 4Rs framework also includes the crucial relationship by which behavioural choices, both positive and negative, result in consequences (rewards and sanctions).

Rights

There are some things which are non-negotiable in an emotionally empowering learning climate. We refer to these as **rights** although they also reflect basic human needs too.

Rights provide a clear rationale for your responses to children's behaviour. They legitimise your intervention and correction as a positive action avoiding the, *'because I said so'* riposte!

The rights approach offers a clear framework to actively teach children to make better choices about their behaviour.

It links back to one of the eight principles, *'Always follow up on issues that count'*. (See page 57)

Rights

The basic rights within a supportive climate are:

1. Everybody's right to safety (physical and psychological)
2. Your right to teach
3. Your children's right to learn
4. Everybody's right to be treated with dignity and respect

Responsibilities

Responsibilities should be clearly linked to the basic rights.

Your key focus should be to persistently and overtly emphasise the connection between protecting rights through personal responsibility.

Put simply, the message is:

> As you have a right to feel safe, you have a responsibility to behave so others can feel the same way too.

Make it clear in all your interactions with children that you will protect the basic rights on their behalf and on your own behalf. However, you will not permit anyone to exercise their rights at the expense of others.

Choices

How do you actually encourage children to accept responsibility?

Effective teachers allow children to make choices about their behaviour. Obviously, these choices are not always conscious choices but it is important to *act as if* they are conscious choices.

The notion of choice is the single most important factor in moving away from unnecessary conflict and confrontation. It distinguishes less effective teachers, who struggle futilely to control children's behaviour, from effective teachers, who seek to influence and then manage the choices children make about their behaviour.

Choices

The benefits of choice:

- It brings empowerment
- It emphasises personal accountability
- It reduces conflict and tension
- It is emotionally consistent with human needs
- It provides a language for managing behaviour

Simply offering children choices does not guarantee that they make socially acceptable ones!

Therefore, choices link tightly to consequences.

Consequences

In a structured climate there can be no 'free' choices. Any choice is bounded by the agenda set.

Perhaps the most influential relationship in creating a positive classroom is that of *inevitability* between choice and consequence.

Practically it operates like this:

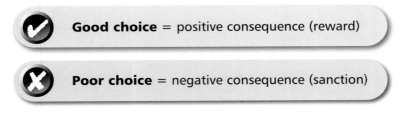

Good choice = positive consequence (reward)

Poor choice = negative consequence (sanction)

Consequences

When applying a reward or a sanction it is crucial to emphasise explicitly that the child is receiving it as a direct result of *their* choice.

There is an important link here to the language of choice (page 46).

When consequences reflect the 'night follows day' principle of inevitability rather than severity, they become hugely influential teaching tools.

Holding children accountable helps you teach them appropriate behaviours and personal responsibility.

Frequent feedback on the positive choices children make is a potent skill that enhances self-esteem and develops personal empowerment.

Rules

It may seem obvious but rules need to make sense to children. Developing your rules within the framework of the 4Rs helps them make sense.

Rules exist in your classroom and around the school simply to protect the basic rights outlined earlier. In this way they are viewed as 'fair' by children who will find it easier to 'buy into' the rules set.

It is good practice to take time to explain the thinking behind your rules to the children to create ownership. It is important to keep the connection between rights and rules.

Display your agreed rules clearly and refer to them regularly as reminders of how to be successful.

Rules

Rules should be:

- Related to the rights/responsibility relationship
- Few in number so everyone can remember them
- Phrased positively (ie what to do rather than what not to do)
- Related to observable behaviours – can you catch them being followed?
- Taught to the children and regularly reinforced

Proactively catching children following the rules and praising them helps to reinforce successful behaviours and to maintain a positive climate in the classroom and beyond.

Routines

Routines are the regular, day-to-day practices that help to keep things running smoothly and effectively.

It is important that routines are actively taught to the children. You will also need to frequently remind them of the routines.

Reinforcing routines offers an opportunity to praise and recognise the positive contribution of the majority of children who consistently do what is expected of them.

Make a deliberate effort to catch groups of children:

- Lining up quietly
- Sitting on the carpet well
- Sharing equipment
- Handling equipment safely

Bringing it all together

The 4Rs is a key feature in the agenda for positively managing behaviour and offers a framework to underpin effective practice.

However, its effectiveness in supporting you and your children in creating a positive learning climate stems from the way in which it is integrated in your daily interactions with children.

The language patterns offered within the 4Rs present you with regular opportunities to remind, reinforce and recognise good practice. These opportunities are at a micro level and form part of every transaction you have with children in and around the classroom.

To develop and embed a culture of success and personal responsibility, you as leader have to 'walk the talk'.

The following pages give you examples of day-to-day language use to embed this crucial organising idea.

Examples of use

'I'm pleased to see everyone protecting safety by wearing goggles. Thanks.'

'Jeff, name calling isn't allowed. We treat each other with respect. Remember that. Thanks.'

'Sheetal, it's your responsibility to get the coursework to me by Friday. How can I help?'

'Nathan, I'd like you to choose to sit down. Thanks.'

'Is everyone in this circle making good choices?'

Examples of use

'Tariq, I love the colours you've chosen in
your painting.'

'Sarah, if you choose not to do your work
now, the consequence will be doing it at
playtime. Make a better choice. Thank
you.'

'Phil, what's our rule about safety?
Use the scissors properly. Thanks.'

'OK. Remind me of the routines for
effective group work. There are three
to remember.'

Result

Because language helps build cultures, the more you use key words in your leadership of your class, the more natural it becomes. The children then accept it as a normal feature of how *we* do things in *our* class.

A Reflective Summary

A reflective summary

The following pages illustrate the features of effective behaviour management. They represent characteristic behaviours and attitudes of effective practitioners, and provide you with a checklist with which to evaluate your practice.

- Make appropriate behaviour your priority
- Establish clear, predictable routines and use them to manage the class
- Actively teach responsibilities
- Model the behaviour and attitude you want to see
- Keep basic respect intact, even when behaviour is unacceptable
- Keep the focus on directing towards successful outcomes

A reflective summary

- Catch them being good
- Give regular, descriptive and positive feedback
- Don't teach students to ignore your directions
- Consciously use body language that conveys authority and confidence
- Use non-confrontational practices
- Give clear choices to encourage ownership of behaviour
- Avoid over-dwelling on behaviours
- Use the least intrusive strategies that are appropriate
- Protect the students' self-esteem
- Separate the behaviour from the person

A reflective summary

- Allow students 'compliance time' to own behaviour and respond
- Follow up incidents with certainty rather than severity
- Re-establish working relationships
- Keep the focus on primary behaviours
- Always correct from the basis of classroom rules
- Avoid using anger as a basis for judgement
- Calm yourself before you calm others

Other reading

Challenging Behaviours Pocketbook
by Fintan O'Regan
Teachers' Pocketbooks, 2006

Classroom Behaviour (3rd Edition)
by Bill Rogers
Sage Publications, 2011

Confident Classroom Leadership
by Hook & Vass
David Fulton Publishers, 2000

Creating Winning Classrooms
by Hook & Vass
David Fulton Publishers, 2000

How to Teach by Phil Beadle
Crown House, 2010

***Managing Very Challenging
Behaviour*** by Louisa Leaman
Continuum Publishing, 2009

Restorative Justice Pocketbook
by M. Thorsborne & D. Vinegrad
Teachers' Pocketbooks, 2009

Teaching with Influence
by Hook & Vass
David Fulton Publishers, 2003

The Art of Teaching Peacefully
by Michelle MacGrath
David Fulton Publishers, 1998

About the authors

Peter Hook

Peter is one of the foremost trainers in behaviour management in the UK. He has developed a national reputation for inspirational and empowering workshops and has worked with over 800 schools, Local Authorities, Educational Services, Connexions Teams and PGCE courses in the past few years. He is both a Member of the Society of Education Consultants and an Affiliate Member of the Chartered Institute of Personnel Development.

Peter has been a consultant to both the DfE and TTA on behaviour management and was responsible for producing the training module for Teaching Assistants launched by the DfE in September 2000. He contributed also to the Key Stage 3 Strategy and is co-author of *'The Coaching & Reflecting Pocketbook'*, *'Confident Classroom Leadership'*, *'Creating Winning Classrooms'* and *'Teaching With Influence'*.

With around 30 years' teaching experience, Peter still regularly works in schools to ensure that the wealth of highly practical strategies he teaches are tested and successful in the reality of today's classrooms.

Peter can be contacted by email: peter@peter-hook.co.uk

or website: www.peterhookassociates.co.uk

About the authors

Andy Vass

Andy has been described by the TES as *'one of the leading trainers in the UK today'*. He has been in education for 35 years and now provides training and coaching to schools, LAs and other organisations both nationally and internationally.

His focus is on empowering staff to build emotionally intelligent learning cultures through excellent communication skills and influential behaviours.

His work and ideas have contributed to National Behaviour Strategy and his reputation is for delivering inspirational, entertaining and hugely practical programmes.

Andy holds postgraduate qualifications in positive psychology, psychotherapy and executive coaching. He has pioneered solution focused approaches and written seven books.

Co-author of *'The Coaching & Reflecting Pocketbook'*, *'Confident Classroom Leadership'*, *'Creating Winning Classrooms'*, *'Teaching with Influence'* and *'Strategies to Close the Learning Gap'*. Sole author of *'Coaching & Mentoring for Leaders'*.

Contact Andy on andy@andyvass.net and view resources and products on www.andyvass.net

Order Form

Your details

Name _____

Position _____

School _____

Address _____

_____

_____

Telephone _____

Fax _____

E-mail _____

VAT No. (EC only) _____

Your Order Ref _____

Please send me:

		No. copies
Behaviour Management	Pocketbook	
_____	Pocketbook	
_____	Pocketbook	
_____	Pocketbook	

Order by Post

Teachers' Pocketbooks
Laurel House, Station Approach
Alresford, Hants. SO24 9JH UK

Order by Phone, Fax or Internet

Telephone: +44 (0)1962 735573
Facsimile: +44 (0)1962 733637
Email: sales@teacherspocketbooks.co.uk
Web: www.teacherspocketbooks.co.uk

Customers in USA should contact:
2427 Bond Street, University Park, IL 60466
Tel: 866 620 6944   Facsimile: 708 534 7803
Email: mp.orders@ware-pak.com
Web: www.teacherspocketbooks.com